HIGH PROTEIN-LOW CARB MASTERPIECES

Delicious, Fat-Burning Recipes for Lean Muscle and Lasting Energy

GLENN DIANNA

Copyright © 2025 Glenn Dianna

All right reserved. No part of this publication may be reproduced, distributed, or transmitted in any form or by any means, including photocopying, recording, or other electronic or mechanical methods, without the prior written permission of the publisher, except in the case of brief quotation embodied in critical reviews and certain other noncommercial uses permitted by copyright law.

Table of Contents

Introduction to HIGH PROTEIN-LOW CARB MASTERPIECES 9

    What's the Buzz About High-Protein, Low-Carb? 10

    Why This Book Will Be Your Go-To Guide 10

    A Journey You Can Stick With 12

The Basics You Need to Know 13

    What's the Deal with High-Protein, Low-Carb? . 13

        How Does It All Fit Together? 15

        Planning Your Meals: Simple, Smart, and Satisfying 17

        Staying on Track: Consistency is Key 18

    Wrapping It Up 19

Foods to Eat and Avoid for a Healthy High-Protein, Low-Carb 20

    Foods to Eat for a High-Protein, Low-Carb 20

        Lean Meats 20

        Fish and Seafood 21

        Eggs 22

        Dairy (in moderation) 22

        Plant-Based Protein Sources 23

        Non-Starchy Vegetables 24

Healthy Fats 25
Foods to Avoid on a High-Protein, Low-Carb Diet
....26
   Refined Carbs and Sugars 26
   High-Carb Grains and Starches........................27
   Fruit (High-Sugar Varieties) 27
   Processed Foods 28
   Alcohol (in excess)...29
In Conclusion 29
Meal Planning for Beginners: High-Protein-Low-Carb Masterpieces Recipes 30
   Why Meal Planning is Essential for Success 30
   Benefits of Meal Planning 31
      Set Your Goals 31
      Choose Your Protein Sources 32
      Add Low-Carb Vegetables 33
      Include Healthy Fats 34
      Choose Your Carb Sources (Smartly)..............35
      Plan for Snacks 36
      Plan Your Meals..36
      Batch Cooking and Prep 37
      Stick to the Plan!...38
   Wrapping Up...38

Comprehensive 7-day High-Protein, Low-Carb meal plan 39
 Day 1 39
  Breakfast: Spinach & Feta Omelet with Avocado 39
  Lunch: Grilled Chicken Salad with Avocado and Olive Oil Dressing 40
  Dinner: Grilled Salmon with Cauliflower Rice and Steamed Broccoli 40
  Snack: Greek Yogurt with Chia Seeds 41
 Day 2 41
  Breakfast: Egg Muffins with Bell Peppers and Cheddar 41
  Lunch: Turkey Lettuce Wraps with Avocado and Tomato 42
  Dinner: Grilled Chicken Thighs with Zucchini Noodles and Pesto 42
  Snack: Boiled Eggs and Celery Sticks 43
 Day 3 43
  Breakfast: Protein Smoothie with Spinach and Almond Butter 43
  Lunch: Tuna Salad with Olive Oil and Avocado 44
  Dinner: Beef Stir-Fry with Bell Peppers and Mushrooms 44

Snack: Cottage Cheese with Sunflower Seeds.45

Day 4 45

   Breakfast: Scrambled Eggs with Bacon and Avocado 45

   Lunch: Chicken Caesar Salad (Low-Carb) 46

   Dinner: Pork Tenderloin with Roasted Brussels Sprouts and Asparagus 46

   Snack: Almonds and Cheese Slices 47

Day 5 48

   Breakfast: Chia Seed Pudding with Almonds and Berries 48

   Lunch: Shrimp & Avocado Salad 48

   Dinner: Grilled Steak with Garlic Butter and Sautéed Spinach 49

   Snack: Celery with Peanut Butter 49

Day 6 50

   Breakfast: Greek Yogurt Parfait with Berries and Walnuts 50

   Lunch: Turkey and Cheese Lettuce Wraps 50

   Dinner: Chicken Stir-Fry with Broccoli and Snow Peas 51

   Snack: Hard-Boiled Eggs 51

Day 7 52

   Breakfast: Avocado & Bacon Egg Cups 52

Lunch: Grilled Salmon Salad with Olive Oil Dressing 52

Dinner: Beef Meatballs with Zucchini Noodles and Marinara Sauce 53

Snack: Cottage Cheese with Berries 53

comprehensive high-protein, low-carb breakfast recipes 55

Spinach & Feta Omelet with Avocado 55

Egg Muffins with Bell Peppers and Cheddar .. 57

Protein Smoothie with Spinach and Almond Butter 58

Scrambled Eggs with Bacon and Avocado 60

Chia Seed Pudding with Almonds and Berrie . 61

Greek Yogurt Parfait with Berries and Walnuts 62

Avocado & Bacon Egg Cups 64

comprehensive high-protein, low-carb lunch recipes 66

Grilled Chicken Salad with Avocado and Olive Oil Dressing 66

Tuna Salad Lettuce Wraps 68

Grilled Salmon with Cauliflower Rice 69

Chicken Caesar Salad (Low-Carb) 71

Beef and Broccoli Stir-Fry 72

- Turkey and Avocado Lettuce Wraps 74
- Shrimp & Avocado Salad 75

Comprehensive high-protein, low-carb dinner recipes...78

- Grilled Salmon with Cauliflower Rice and Steamed Broccoli 78
- Chicken Thighs with Roasted Brussels Sprouts and Asparagus 80
- Beef Stir-Fry with Bell Peppers and Snow Peas 81
- Grilled Chicken with Zucchini Noodles and Pesto..83
- Baked Cod with Roasted Cauliflower and Spinach 85
- Shrimp and Avocado Salad with Lime Dressing 87
- Pork Tenderloin with Roasted Green Beans and Mushrooms..89

Conclusion: Embrace the High-Protein, Low-Carb Lifestyle with Confidence 91

INTRODUCTION TO HIGH PROTEIN-LOW CARB MASTERPIECES

Welcome to **High Protein-Low Carb Masterpieces**, where great taste and health meet in the perfect balance. Whether you're new to the world of high-protein, low-carb eating or you've been experimenting for a while, this book is designed to guide you step by step through the process of adopting a lifestyle that works not just for your body but for your overall well-being.

Let's face it—eating healthy can sometimes feel like a chore. But here, we're flipping the script. Gone are the days of bland, flavorless meals that leave you feeling unsatisfied. Instead, we're bringing you a collection of recipes that are not only delicious but packed with all the nutrients your body craves. From energizing breakfasts to satisfying lunches, indulgent dinners, and snacks you'll actually look forward to—this book is your ticket to flavorful meals that align with your goals.

WHAT'S THE BUZZ ABOUT HIGH-PROTEIN, LOW-CARB?

By now, you've probably heard a lot about high-protein, low-carb diets. But what exactly does that mean for you? The simple answer is this: cutting down on carbs while increasing your protein intake can support a range of benefits—from weight management to muscle building, and even boosting your metabolism. It's a lifestyle that has stood the test of time, embraced by athletes, health enthusiasts, and anyone looking to feel more energetic and nourished.

However, the idea of cutting out certain foods or adjusting your routine can feel overwhelming at first. The good news is that with the right approach, this way of eating doesn't need to be a struggle. In fact, it can be an exciting journey where you discover new ways to make delicious meals while achieving your health and fitness goals.

WHY THIS BOOK WILL BE YOUR GO-TO GUIDE

In **High Protein-Low Carb Masterpieces**, I've carefully curated recipes that are easy to follow, packed with flavor, and designed for long-term success. Each recipe has been crafted to ensure you don't miss out on the nutrients your body needs, while keeping carbs in check. Whether you're cooking for one, meal prepping for the week, or feeding a family, you'll find that these meals are as versatile as they are satisfying.

But this book isn't just about recipes—it's about a lifestyle. Throughout the pages, you'll find:

- **Meal Planning Tips**: Learn how to plan your meals, create a shopping list, and prep like a pro. With a little strategy, you can set yourself up for success all week long.

- **Nutritional Guidance**: No need to stress about counting every calorie or carb—this book helps you understand what goes into each meal, empowering you to make informed decisions without feeling overwhelmed.

- **Sustaining Consistency**: One of the most challenging parts of any lifestyle change is staying consistent. We'll share tips and tricks to keep you motivated and focused, even when life gets busy.

- **Creative, Flavorful Recipes**: Say goodbye to boring meals! From savory breakfasts like egg muffins and protein-packed smoothies to hearty dinners such as grilled chicken with zesty cauliflower rice, each dish is crafted to satisfy both your hunger and your taste buds.

I'll also be diving into the science behind high-protein, low-carb eating, so you can understand why this approach works and how to make it a natural part of your daily life. And don't worry if you're not a seasoned chef—these recipes are designed with ease in mind, whether you're an experienced cook or just getting started in the kitchen.

A JOURNEY YOU CAN STICK WITH

This isn't a crash diet or a temporary fix; it's a sustainable way of living. It's about making mindful choices, enjoying what you eat, and feeling good about the food you're fueling your body with. If you're ready to unlock the power of high-protein, low-carb eating while enjoying every meal along the way, then you're in the right place.

Get ready to transform your relationship with food. Let's dive into the mouthwatering, nourishing world of **High Protein-Low Carb Masterpieces**. You won't just be following a diet—you'll be embracing a lifestyle that brings out the best in you, one delicious recipe at a time.

Ready to cook up some masterpieces? Let's begin.

THE BASICS YOU NEED TO KNOW

So, you've heard the buzz about high-protein, low-carb eating and maybe you're wondering what all the hype is about. Is it really as good as people say? How can it work for me? And more importantly, how can you make it delicious and sustainable, without feeling like you're depriving yourself?

Let's break it down together and walk through this in a way that makes sense. After all, eating well is about making choices that fit into your life—not about pushing yourself into some rigid, uncomfortable routine. So, grab a cup of tea (or coffee if that's your thing), and let's dive into the foundations of a high-protein, low-carb lifestyle.

WHAT'S THE DEAL WITH HIGH-PROTEIN, LOW-CARB?

At its core, a high-protein, low-carb diet focuses on shifting the balance of what you eat. Instead of filling up on foods like pasta, bread, or sugary treats (we know they're tempting!), you fill your plate with lean meats, fish, eggs, nuts, seeds, and plenty of colorful vegetables. By doing this, you reduce your carbohydrate intake, which can help your body burn fat more efficiently and support muscle growth.

Let's get a little deeper into this. When you eat a meal that's high in protein and low in carbs, your body experiences a few key benefits:

1. **Stable Blood Sugar Levels**: Carbs, especially refined ones, can spike your blood sugar and lead to crashes. By reducing carbs and increasing protein, you stabilize your blood sugar, which means fewer cravings and more consistent energy levels throughout the day. No more feeling sluggish or battling mid-afternoon crashes.

2. **Increased Muscle Mass**: Protein is the building block of muscle, and consuming more of it helps your body repair and build muscle tissue. Whether you're working out regularly or just want to feel more toned and strong, a high-protein diet can support those goals.

3. **Enhanced Fat Burning**: The magic behind the low-carb aspect of this diet is that it encourages your body to use stored fat for fuel instead of relying on glucose from carbs. Essentially, you start burning fat for energy, which helps with weight management or fat loss—without the hunger or deprivation.

4. **Better Satiety**: Protein-rich foods are incredibly filling, so you feel fuller for longer. This means you're less likely to snack on unhealthy foods throughout the day. It's like hitting two birds with one stone—less hunger and fewer cravings.

HOW DOES IT ALL FIT TOGETHER?

By now, you're probably thinking, "This all sounds great, but how do I make it work in real life?" And that's the beauty of this lifestyle—it's not about drastic changes; it's about making small, manageable shifts.

Here's how to start:

1. **Focus on Protein**: Protein should be the star of your meals. Think about incorporating lean meats (like chicken or turkey), fish, eggs, and plant-based proteins (like tofu or tempeh) into each meal. A protein-rich meal will not only help with muscle growth but also keep you feeling full, so you can enjoy fewer snacks in between meals.

2. **Cut Down on Refined Carbs**: It's not about cutting out all carbs completely

(because let's face it, who can live without their morning toast every now and then?), but it's about making smarter choices. Instead of white bread or sugary snacks, opt for whole grains, leafy greens, or cauliflower rice. These foods are lower in carbs but still rich in fiber, so they'll help keep your digestion healthy and keep you satisfied.

3. **Healthy Fats are Your Friend**: Don't shy away from healthy fats like avocado, olive oil, or fatty fish like salmon. These fats can actually help with fat loss, support your brain health, and give your meals that extra flavor boost you crave.

4. **Vegetables are Essential**: Never underestimate the power of vegetables! Low-carb, high-fiber vegetables are the perfect accompaniment to any meal. Think leafy greens like spinach and kale, cruciferous veggies like broccoli and cauliflower, and colorful peppers and zucchini. They're low in carbs but packed with nutrients, making them the ideal foundation for any meal.

PLANNING YOUR MEALS: SIMPLE, SMART, AND SATISFYING

One of the most important things about starting this journey is to make meal planning a habit. I know it might sound a bit overwhelming at first, but it doesn't have to be. In fact, meal planning can actually make your life a whole lot easier by ensuring that you always have nutritious, high-protein, low-carb meals at your fingertips.

Here's a basic strategy for meal planning:

1. **Plan Around Protein**: Start by picking your protein source for each meal. If you know you'll have chicken for dinner, then you can plan sides around that. Maybe a fresh green salad with avocado or roasted vegetables. If you prefer a plant-based option, tofu stir-fried with broccoli and a little sesame oil could be just as satisfying.

2. **Get Creative with Leftovers**: Leftovers are your best friend. You can take yesterday's grilled chicken and turn it into a hearty salad or mix it into a low-carb wrap for lunch. That way, you're saving time and making sure your meals are balanced.

3. **Batch Cook When You Can**: Sundays are a great day to prep. Cook up a big batch of protein—like grilled chicken, roasted salmon, or boiled eggs—so you have a base ready to go. Then, when it's time for meals, just grab and assemble.

4. **Snack Smart**: When hunger strikes between meals, make sure you have high-protein, low-carb snacks on hand. Think nuts, boiled eggs, cheese sticks, or a protein smoothie. These snacks will help you stay on track without the temptation of high-carb, sugary options.

STAYING ON TRACK: CONSISTENCY IS KEY

As with any lifestyle change, the key to success is consistency. It's easy to get excited in the beginning, but staying committed over time is where the real transformation happens. Here are a few tips to help you stay on track:

- **Don't Be Too Hard on Yourself**: If you have a slice of pizza or some fries, it's okay. The goal is progress, not perfection. Just get back to your high-protein, low-carb meals the next day and keep going.

- **Celebrate Small Wins**: Every time you feel more energized, notice your clothes fitting better, or realize you've made it through the day without a sugar crash, celebrate it! These little victories are what add up to big changes.

- **Find Your Support**: Share your goals with friends or family who can support you along the way. You could even join a community of like-minded people who are also making this lifestyle work for them. Having a support system can be the difference between success and giving up.

WRAPPING IT UP

This isn't a quick-fix diet; it's a way of life that, with time, can help you feel stronger, healthier, and more energized. And the best part? You don't have to sacrifice taste to get there. With the right recipes, tips, and mindset, you'll find that eating high-protein, low-carb meals is not just sustainable—it's downright enjoyable. So, as you flip through the pages of this book, keep in mind that this is just the beginning of your flavorful journey. Let's make every meal a masterpiece!

Now, grab your apron and let's get cooking.

FOODS TO EAT AND AVOID FOR A HEALTHY HIGH-PROTEIN, LOW-CARB

When it comes to a high-protein, low-carb lifestyle, the food choices you make are crucial for your success. The goal is to fuel your body with protein-rich, low-carb foods that promote health, energy, and sustained weight management while avoiding foods that might derail your progress.

Let's break down what to eat and what to avoid so you can make smart, delicious choices every time you sit down to a meal.

FOODS TO EAT FOR A HIGH-PROTEIN, LOW-CARB

LEAN MEATS

Protein is your best friend in this lifestyle, and lean meats are one of the richest sources of it.

The key here is choosing meats that are low in fat and full of high-quality protein.

- **Chicken breast**
- **Turkey**
- **Lean cuts of beef** (e.g., sirloin, round steak)
- **Pork tenderloin**
- **Lamb**

These meats are packed with protein to keep you feeling full while keeping your carb intake low. Opt for skinless poultry and trim any visible fat from cuts of beef or pork to keep them lean.

FISH AND SEAFOOD

Fish is another excellent source of protein, and it's full of healthy fats like omega-3s, which can help improve heart health and reduce inflammation. Seafood also tends to be very low in carbs.

- **Salmon**
- **Tuna**
- **Mackerel**
- **Sardines**

- **Shrimp**
- **Cod**

Aim to eat a variety of fish a few times a week to get the benefits of both protein and heart-healthy fats.

EGGS

Eggs are an incredible source of high-quality protein, packed with essential nutrients like vitamins A, D, and B12. The best part? They're extremely versatile and can be enjoyed in so many ways.

- **Boiled eggs**
- **Scrambled eggs**
- **Egg muffins**
- **Omelets**

Eggs can be included in nearly every meal—whether you have them for breakfast, lunch, or dinner.

DAIRY (IN MODERATION)

Dairy products can be a great source of protein, but not all dairy is created equal. Go for the full-fat, unsweetened varieties to keep carbs in check.

- **Greek yogurt (unsweetened)**
- **Cottage cheese**
- **Hard cheeses** (cheddar, mozzarella, parmesan)
- **Heavy cream** (used in small amounts for cooking)

These options will give you that creamy, delicious texture you crave while keeping your protein high and carbs low. Just be cautious of flavored yogurts or dairy products that contain added sugars.

PLANT-BASED PROTEIN SOURCES

If you prefer plant-based options, there are plenty of high-protein, low-carb alternatives to consider.

- **Tofu**
- **Tempeh**
- **Seitan**
- **Edamame**
- **Lentils** (in moderation, as they are higher in carbs but still provide protein)

These can be fantastic additions to stir-fries, salads, and bowls. Just be mindful of your portion sizes for lentils or other legumes to keep your carb count in check.

NON-STARCHY VEGETABLES

Vegetables are an essential part of any healthy diet, and for a high-protein, low-carb lifestyle, you'll want to focus on non-starchy, low-carb veggies that provide plenty of fiber, vitamins, and minerals.

- **Spinach**
- **Kale**
- **Broccoli**
- **Cauliflower**
- **Zucchini**
- **Cucumbers**
- **Bell peppers**
- **Mushrooms**
- **Asparagus**

These vegetables are low in carbs, so you can eat them in large quantities without worrying about breaking your carb limit.

HEALTHY FATS

Healthy fats are an important component of the high-protein, low-carb lifestyle because they help keep you satisfied and support your body's nutrient absorption.

- **Avocado**
- **Olive oil**
- **Coconut oil**
- **Nuts and seeds** (almonds, chia seeds, flaxseeds, walnuts, sunflower seeds)

These fats also provide anti-inflammatory benefits and are great for cooking, drizzling on salads, or snacking.

2. **Berries (in moderation)**
   When it comes to fruit, most fruits are higher in carbs due to their sugar content. However, berries are lower in carbs compared to other fruits, making them a great option for satisfying your sweet tooth while staying within your carb limits.

   - **Strawberries**
   - **Blueberries**

- **Blackberries**
- **Raspberries**

A handful of berries can be a refreshing, nutrient-packed addition to your meals or snacks.

FOODS TO AVOID ON A HIGH-PROTEIN, LOW-CARB DIET

REFINED CARBS AND SUGARS

These are the main culprits when it comes to spiking your blood sugar and derailing your efforts to stay in fat-burning mode. Avoid foods like:

- **White bread**
- **Pastries and cakes**
- **Candy and sweets**
- **Sugary breakfast cereals**
- **Soda and sweetened drinks**

These foods not only add unnecessary carbs but also provide very little nutritional value. Instead, opt for whole-food alternatives like low-carb wraps or sugar-free desserts when you need something sweet.

HIGH-CARB GRAINS AND STARCHES

While grains and starches can be part of a healthy diet, they're higher in carbs and should be limited on a high-protein, low-carb plan.

- **White rice**
- **Pasta**
- **Potatoes**
- **Corn**
- **Bagels**

Consider swapping these out for cauliflower rice, zucchini noodles, or spaghetti squash, which are all great low-carb alternatives.

FRUIT (HIGH-SUGAR VARIETIES)

While fruits like berries are a great low-carb option, other fruits are higher in sugars and carbs, so they're best avoided or consumed in moderation.

- **Bananas**
- **Apples**
- **Pineapple**
- **Grapes**
- **Mangoes**

If you're craving fruit, stick to small portions of berries or citrus fruits like lemons and limes.

PROCESSED FOODS

Many processed foods contain hidden sugars, unhealthy fats, and refined carbs that can throw off your progress. Avoid:

- **Processed snacks (chips, cookies, crackers)**
- **Fast food**
- **Pre-packaged meals**
- **Sugary sauces and dressings** (like ketchup or BBQ sauce)

Opt for homemade meals or minimally processed options when possible. It's always better to control what goes into your food.

ALCOHOL (IN EXCESS)

While the occasional glass of wine or a light beer is okay, alcohol can be high in sugar and empty calories, which can hinder your goals. Plus, alcohol can increase cravings and decrease your willpower when it comes to making healthy food choices. If you do drink, choose dry wine or spirits (like vodka or whiskey) mixed with sparkling water or a sugar-free soda.

IN CONCLUSION

Adopting a high-protein, low-carb lifestyle is all about making the right choices—choosing foods that nourish your body and support your health goals while cutting back on foods that can hinder your progress. By focusing on lean proteins, healthy fats, and low-carb vegetables, you'll have a diet that not only supports weight loss and muscle gain but also keeps you feeling energized and satisfied throughout the day.

Remember, it's about balance. While you focus on eating high-protein, low-carb foods, there's no need to deprive yourself—just make smarter choices that align with your goals. The more you practice, the easier it becomes to create meals that are both nourishing and delicious.

MEAL PLANNING FOR BEGINNERS: HIGH-PROTEIN-LOW-CARB MASTERPIECES RECIPES

If you're new to the high-protein, low-carb lifestyle, meal planning might seem a bit daunting at first. But don't worry—meal planning doesn't need to be complicated or time-consuming. In fact, with a little strategy and a few key steps, you can set yourself up for success and make your journey to a healthier lifestyle enjoyable and sustainable.

Let's break it down together, step by step, so you can create delicious, nutritious meals without the stress.

WHY MEAL PLANNING IS ESSENTIAL FOR SUCCESS

Meal planning is an absolute game-changer when it comes to sticking with a high-protein, low-carb diet. When you plan ahead, you ensure that your meals are balanced, your shopping is efficient, and your days run smoother. It also helps you avoid last-minute temptations to grab something unhealthy because you'll already have everything ready to go.

BENEFITS OF MEAL PLANNING

- **Saves Time**: Having meals prepped and ready to go means no scrambling for something to eat at the last minute.

- **Reduces Stress**: No more "What's for dinner tonight?" moments. Your meals are already planned out.

- **Prevents Overeating**: When you have healthy, protein-packed meals ready, you're less likely to snack on high-carb, sugary foods.

- **Budget-Friendly**: Meal planning can help you avoid food waste and overspending by ensuring you only buy what you need.

SET YOUR GOALS

Before you start planning, take a moment to reflect on your personal goals. Are you looking to lose weight? Build muscle? Or simply maintain a healthy, balanced lifestyle? Knowing your goals will help shape your meal choices. For example:

- **Weight loss**: Focus on meals that are lower in calories while still being high in protein to keep you full.
- **Muscle building**: You'll want to eat more protein-rich foods and might also need slightly higher calories to support muscle growth.
- **Overall health**: A balanced approach where protein is prioritized, carbs are controlled, and you get plenty of healthy fats.

Once you know your goals, meal planning becomes much easier because you'll have a clearer sense of what to prioritize.

CHOOSE YOUR PROTEIN SOURCES

Protein is the foundation of your high-protein, low-carb meals. So, start by picking your protein sources. As a beginner, it's helpful to focus on simple, versatile proteins that can be used in a variety of dishes. Here are some options:

- **Chicken breast**

- **Turkey**
- **Fish** (like salmon or tuna)
- **Eggs**
- **Greek yogurt** (unsweetened)
- **Tofu or tempeh** (for plant-based options)

When planning, aim to have a protein source in every meal—whether that's a breakfast scramble, a chicken salad for lunch, or grilled fish for dinner.

ADD LOW-CARB VEGETABLES

Vegetables are the perfect complement to your high-protein meals. They're low in carbs, rich in fiber, and packed with vitamins and minerals that your body needs to stay healthy. When meal planning, aim to fill half of your plate with non-starchy vegetables. Here are some great options:

- **Leafy greens** (spinach, kale, arugula)
- **Cruciferous vegetables** (broccoli, cauliflower, Brussels sprouts)
- **Zucchini, cucumbers, bell peppers, mushrooms**
- **Asparagus, green beans, and cabbage**

These veggies can be eaten raw, sautéed, roasted, or steamed. They add bulk to your meals, helping you feel full while keeping carbs low.

INCLUDE HEALTHY FATS

Healthy fats are important because they help you stay satisfied, support your metabolism, and provide essential nutrients. You don't need a lot of fat, but a few healthy fats in each meal will make your dishes more satisfying and help you stay energized throughout the day. Here are some great options to include:

- **Avocado** (perfect for salads, bowls, or as a topping)
- **Olive oil** or **coconut oil** (for cooking or drizzling on vegetables)
- **Nuts and seeds** (almonds, chia seeds, flaxseeds, walnuts)
- **Fatty fish** (like salmon or sardines)

Be mindful of portion sizes with fats, as they are calorie-dense, but don't skip them—they'll help keep you satisfied and support your body's fat-burning processes.

CHOOSE YOUR CARB SOURCES (SMARTLY)

Since this is a low-carb lifestyle, you don't need to load up on carbs, but you will want to include some carbs that are nutrient-dense and come from whole food sources. These carbs will be lower in sugar and packed with fiber, which helps regulate digestion and keep you full. Here's where you can focus:

- **Non-starchy vegetables** (as mentioned above)
- **Small portions of high-fiber fruits** like berries (strawberries, raspberries, blueberries)
- **Whole grains (if your carb tolerance allows)** like quinoa or brown rice
- **Legumes** like lentils or chickpeas (in moderation)

It's important to pay attention to your portions here. You're aiming for **low-carb**, not no-carb, so choosing the right carbs and watching your portion sizes will help you stay on track.

PLAN FOR SNACKS

Snacking on a high-protein, low-carb lifestyle can actually be really enjoyable—if you have the right snacks on hand. Healthy snacks will keep you from reaching for carb-heavy, sugary options when you're hungry. Here are a few snack ideas:

- **Boiled eggs**
- **Greek yogurt (unsweetened)** with a sprinkle of chia seeds or a handful of berries
- **Nuts and seeds** (almonds, walnuts, sunflower seeds)
- **Cottage cheese** with a few slices of cucumber or cherry tomatoes
- **Protein shakes** (especially after a workout)
- **Cheese sticks** or slices of hard cheese

By planning ahead and keeping your snacks protein-packed and low in carbs, you'll avoid the temptation of processed or sugary foods.

PLAN YOUR MEALS

Now that you know your protein sources, vegetables, fats, and low-carb carbs, it's time to start planning your meals for the week. Here's how you can structure it:

- **Breakfast**: Think protein-rich options like scrambled eggs with spinach and avocado, or a protein smoothie made with Greek yogurt, almond milk, and berries.

- **Lunch**: Focus on a lean protein (grilled chicken, tuna, or tofu) with a big serving of vegetables (like a mixed green salad with olive oil and avocado).

- **Dinner**: A lean protein with roasted non-starchy vegetables (like baked salmon with broccoli or a grilled steak with sautéed mushrooms).

- **Snacks**: Keep it simple with snacks like boiled eggs, nuts, or a small portion of Greek yogurt with a few berries.

BATCH COOKING AND PREP

For the best results, consider preparing some ingredients in bulk. This saves time and ensures you have healthy meals ready to go. You can grill chicken breasts, roast a batch of vegetables, or make a big pot of quinoa or cauliflower rice to use throughout the week.

Batch cooking can be a game-changer—make a big pot of soup, grill a bunch of fish or meat, or prepare a few salads to take with you. With everything prepped, all you have to do is assemble when it's time to eat.

STICK TO THE PLAN!

Meal planning only works if you stick to it. Be flexible if things don't go exactly as planned, but stay committed to your goals. If life gets in the way, there's always the option of leftovers or simple protein options like boiled eggs, yogurt, or quick stir-fries with leftover vegetables.

WRAPPING UP

Meal planning for a high-protein, low-carb lifestyle doesn't have to be stressful—it's all about keeping things simple, focusing on quality ingredients, and creating balanced meals that support your health goals. Start small, plan ahead, and soon enough, you'll be a pro at making healthy, delicious meals that fuel your body and fit perfectly into your lifestyle.

Remember, this is about making changes that work for *you*, so don't rush it. The more you plan, the easier it gets. Enjoy the process, and know that you're on the path to healthier, more vibrant living with every meal you create.

COMPREHENSIVE 7-DAY HIGH-PROTEIN, LOW-CARB MEAL PLAN

DAY 1

BREAKFAST:
SPINACH & FETA OMELET WITH AVOCADO

- 3 large eggs
- Handful of spinach
- 2 tbsp crumbled feta cheese
- 1/4 avocado, sliced
- Salt and pepper to taste
  Instructions: Whisk eggs, sauté spinach in olive oil, and pour the eggs over. Add feta, cook, and fold. Serve with fresh avocado slices on top.

LUNCH:
GRILLED CHICKEN SALAD WITH AVOCADO AND OLIVE OIL DRESSING

- 4 oz grilled chicken breast
- Mixed greens (spinach, arugula, lettuce)
- 1/4 avocado, sliced
- Cherry tomatoes, cucumber, and red onion
- 2 tbsp olive oil
- 1 tbsp balsamic vinegar
- Salt and pepper to taste
  Instructions: Toss all veggies in a large bowl. Top with sliced chicken breast, drizzle with olive oil and balsamic vinegar, and season to taste.

DINNER:
GRILLED SALMON WITH CAULIFLOWER RICE AND STEAMED BROCCOLI

- 6 oz salmon fillet

- 1 cup cauliflower rice
- 1 cup steamed broccoli
- 1 tbsp olive oil
  Instructions: Grill salmon, sauté cauliflower rice in olive oil, and steam the broccoli. Serve salmon on top of the cauliflower rice and broccoli.

SNACK: GREEK YOGURT WITH CHIA SEEDS

- 1/2 cup unsweetened Greek yogurt
- 1 tbsp chia seeds
  Instructions: Mix chia seeds into the yogurt for a protein-packed snack.

DAY 2

BREAKFAST: EGG MUFFINS WITH BELL PEPPERS AND CHEDDAR

- 3 large eggs
- 1/2 cup diced bell peppers

- 2 tbsp shredded cheddar cheese
- Salt and pepper to taste
  Instructions: Whisk eggs and pour into muffin tin. Add diced peppers and cheese. Bake at 375°F (190°C) for 20-25 minutes.

LUNCH:
TURKEY LETTUCE WRAPS WITH AVOCADO AND TOMATO

- 4 oz sliced turkey breast
- 2 large romaine lettuce leaves
- 1/4 avocado, sliced
- 2 tomato slices
- Mustard or mayonnaise (optional)
  Instructions: Layer turkey slices, avocado, and tomato on lettuce leaves. Wrap up and enjoy!

DINNER:
GRILLED CHICKEN THIGHS WITH ZUCCHINI NOODLES AND PESTO

- 6 oz chicken thighs

- 2 cups zucchini noodles
- 2 tbsp pesto sauce
  Instructions: Grill chicken thighs. Sauté zucchini noodles in a little olive oil, then toss with pesto sauce. Serve with chicken.

SNACK:
BOILED EGGS AND CELERY STICKS

- 2 boiled eggs
- Celery sticks
  Instructions: Peel the boiled eggs and enjoy with fresh celery.

DAY 3

BREAKFAST:
PROTEIN SMOOTHIE WITH SPINACH AND ALMOND BUTTER

- 1 scoop protein powder (low-carb)
- 1 cup unsweetened almond milk

- 1/2 cup spinach
- 1 tbsp almond butter
- Ice cubes
  Instructions: Blend all ingredients until smooth and creamy.

LUNCH:
TUNA SALAD WITH OLIVE OIL AND AVOCADO

- 1 can tuna (in water, drained)
- 1/4 avocado, mashed
- 2 tbsp olive oil
- 1 tbsp lemon juice
- Salt and pepper to taste
  Instructions: Mix tuna with avocado, olive oil, and lemon juice. Season with salt and pepper. Serve on top of a bed of lettuce or in a low-carb wrap.

DINNER:
BEEF STIR-FRY WITH BELL PEPPERS AND MUSHROOMS

- 6 oz lean beef (flank steak or sirloin)

- 1 cup bell peppers, sliced
- 1/2 cup mushrooms, sliced
- 2 tbsp soy sauce (or coconut aminos)
- 1 tbsp olive oil
  Instructions: Stir-fry beef in olive oil, add veggies and soy sauce, and cook until tender.

SNACK: COTTAGE CHEESE WITH SUNFLOWER SEEDS

- 1/2 cup cottage cheese
- 1 tbsp sunflower seeds
  Instructions: Mix sunflower seeds into cottage cheese for a satisfying snack.

DAY 4

BREAKFAST: SCRAMBLED EGGS WITH BACON AND AVOCADO

- 3 large eggs
- 2 slices turkey bacon

- 1/4 avocado, sliced
  Instructions: Scramble eggs and cook turkey bacon. Serve eggs with bacon and avocado on the side.

LUNCH:
CHICKEN CAESAR SALAD (LOW-CARB)

- 4 oz grilled chicken breast
- Romaine lettuce
- 2 tbsp homemade Caesar dressing (no sugar)
- Parmesan cheese
  Instructions: Toss chicken and lettuce in Caesar dressing. Top with Parmesan.

DINNER:
PORK TENDERLOIN WITH ROASTED BRUSSELS SPROUTS AND ASPARAGUS

- 6 oz pork tenderloin
- 1 cup Brussels sprouts, halved
- 1 cup asparagus spears

- 1 tbsp olive oil
  Instructions: Roast Brussels sprouts and asparagus in olive oil at 400°F (200°C) for 20-25 minutes. Grill pork tenderloin and serve with roasted vegetables.

SNACK:
ALMONDS AND CHEESE SLICES

- 1 oz almonds
- 2 slices cheese (cheddar or mozzarella)
  Instructions: Enjoy a handful of almonds and cheese slices for a satisfying snack.

DAY 5

BREAKFAST:
CHIA SEED PUDDING WITH ALMONDS AND BERRIES

- 2 tbsp chia seeds
- 1/2 cup unsweetened almond milk
- 1/4 cup mixed berries
- 1 tbsp sliced almonds
  Instructions: Mix chia seeds and almond milk. Let sit overnight. Top with berries and almonds before serving.

LUNCH:
SHRIMP & AVOCADO SALAD

- 4 oz shrimp, cooked
- Mixed greens (arugula, spinach)
- 1/4 avocado, sliced
- Cucumber and red onion
- Olive oil and lemon dressing
  Instructions: Toss all ingredients together with olive oil and lemon juice.

DINNER: GRILLED STEAK WITH GARLIC BUTTER AND SAUTÉED SPINACH

- 6 oz ribeye or sirloin steak
- 1 tbsp butter
- 2 cups spinach
  Instructions: Grill steak to desired doneness. In a pan, sauté spinach with butter and garlic until wilted. Top steak with garlic butter.

SNACK: CELERY WITH PEANUT BUTTER

- 2 celery sticks
- 1 tbsp natural peanut butter
  Instructions: Spread peanut butter onto celery sticks for a crunchy, satisfying snack.

DAY 6

BREAKFAST:
GREEK YOGURT PARFAIT WITH BERRIES AND WALNUTS

- 1/2 cup unsweetened Greek yogurt
- 1/4 cup mixed berries
- 1 tbsp chopped walnuts
  Instructions: Layer Greek yogurt with berries and walnuts in a parfait glass.

LUNCH:
TURKEY AND CHEESE LETTUCE WRAPS

- 4 oz sliced turkey breast
- 2 large lettuce leaves
- 1 slice cheese (Swiss or cheddar)
- Mustard or mayo (optional)
  Instructions: Layer turkey, cheese, and mustard or mayo on lettuce leaves and wrap up.

DINNER: CHICKEN STIR-FRY WITH BROCCOLI AND SNOW PEAS

- 6 oz chicken breast, cubed
- 1 cup broccoli florets
- 1/2 cup snow peas
- 2 tbsp soy sauce (or coconut aminos)
- 1 tbsp sesame oil
  Instructions: Stir-fry chicken in sesame oil, add vegetables and soy sauce, and cook until tender.

SNACK: HARD-BOILED EGGS

- 2 hard-boiled eggs
  Instructions: Enjoy two hard-boiled eggs for a simple, protein-packed snack.

DAY 7

BREAKFAST:
AVOCADO & BACON EGG CUPS

- 2 large eggs
- 2 slices turkey bacon
- 1/4 avocado, diced
  Instructions: Bake eggs in avocado halves at 375°F (190°C) for 15 minutes. Top with crispy bacon.

LUNCH:
GRILLED SALMON SALAD WITH OLIVE OIL DRESSING

- 4 oz grilled salmon
- Mixed greens
- Cherry tomatoes, cucumber, and red onion
- Olive oil and lemon dressing
  Instructions: Toss salad ingredients together and top with grilled salmon and dressing.

DINNER: BEEF MEATBALLS WITH ZUCCHINI NOODLES AND MARINARA SAUCE

- 6 oz ground beef (or turkey)
- 1/2 cup marinara sauce (low-carb)
- 2 cups zucchini noodles
- 1 tbsp olive oil
  Instructions: Form beef into meatballs and bake at 375°F (190°C) for 20 minutes. Sauté zucchini noodles and top with marinara sauce and meatballs.

SNACK: COTTAGE CHEESE WITH BERRIES

- 1/2 cup cottage cheese
- 1/4 cup mixed berries
  Instructions: Mix berries into cottage cheese for a sweet and savory snack.

This meal plan gives you a variety of high-protein, low-carb meals throughout the week, keeping things fresh, flavorful, and satisfying. You can customize the plan further based on your preferences, but this will give you a strong foundation to start your high-protein, low-carb journey! Enjoy.

COMPREHENSIVE HIGH-PROTEIN, LOW-CARB BREAKFAST RECIPES

SPINACH & FETA OMELET WITH AVOCADO

Ingredients:

- 3 large eggs
- 1/2 cup fresh spinach, chopped
- 2 tbsp crumbled feta cheese
- 1/4 avocado, sliced
- 1 tbsp olive oil
- Salt and pepper to taste

Instructions:

1. Heat olive oil in a non-stick skillet over medium heat.

2. Add chopped spinach and sauté until wilted, about 2 minutes.
3. Whisk eggs with a pinch of salt and pepper, then pour over spinach.
4. Sprinkle feta cheese evenly over eggs.
5. Cook for about 3-4 minutes until eggs set, then fold the omelet in half.
6. Serve with sliced avocado on top.

Cooking Time: 5 minutes
Prep Time: 5 minutes
Servings: 1

Nutritional Information (per serving):

- Calories: 350
- Protein: 24g
- Carbs: 6g
- Fiber: 3g
- Fat: 26g
- Sugar: 2g

EGG MUFFINS WITH BELL PEPPERS AND CHEDDAR

Ingredients:

- 4 large eggs
- 1/2 cup diced bell peppers (mix of red, yellow, and green)
- 2 tbsp shredded cheddar cheese
- 1 tbsp olive oil
- Salt and pepper to taste

Instructions:

1. Preheat the oven to 375°F (190°C).
2. Grease a muffin tin with olive oil or cooking spray.
3. In a bowl, whisk eggs and season with salt and pepper.
4. Add diced bell peppers and cheddar cheese to the eggs.
5. Pour the egg mixture evenly into the muffin tin, filling each cup about 3/4 full.
6. Bake for 18-20 minutes, or until eggs are set and lightly golden on top.

7. Let cool slightly before removing from the muffin tin.

Cooking Time: 20 minutes
Prep Time: 5 minutes
Servings: 4 (1 muffin per serving)

Nutritional Information (per muffin):

- Calories: 150
- Protein: 9g
- Carbs: 2g
- Fiber: 1g
- Fat: 12g
- Sugar: 1g

PROTEIN SMOOTHIE WITH SPINACH AND ALMOND BUTTER

Ingredients:

- 1 scoop protein powder (low-carb, vanilla or chocolate flavor)
- 1 cup unsweetened almond milk

- 1/2 cup fresh spinach
- 1 tbsp almond butter
- Ice cubes

Instructions:

1. Add almond milk, spinach, protein powder, and almond butter to a blender.
2. Blend until smooth and creamy. Add ice cubes and blend again for a thicker consistency.
3. Pour into a glass and enjoy immediately.

Cooking Time: 1 minute
Prep Time: 2 minutes
Servings: 1

Nutritional Information (per serving):

- Calories: 300
- Protein: 25g
- Carbs: 7g
- Fiber: 3g
- Fat: 18g
- Sugar: 3g

SCRAMBLED EGGS WITH BACON AND AVOCADO

Ingredients:

- 3 large eggs
- 2 slices turkey bacon
- 1/4 avocado, sliced
- Salt and pepper to taste

Instructions:

1. Heat a pan over medium heat and cook the turkey bacon until crispy, about 5-6 minutes. Set aside.
2. In the same pan, scramble the eggs with a pinch of salt and pepper. Cook for 2-3 minutes until eggs are cooked through.
3. Serve the scrambled eggs with crispy bacon and sliced avocado on the side.

Cooking Time: 10 minutes
Prep Time: 3 minutes
Servings: 1

Nutritional Information (per serving):

- Calories: 320
- Protein: 26g
- Carbs: 6g
- Fiber: 4g
- Fat: 24g
- Sugar: 1g

CHIA SEED PUDDING WITH ALMONDS AND BERRIES

Ingredients:

- 2 tbsp chia seeds
- 1/2 cup unsweetened almond milk
- 1/4 cup mixed berries (blueberries, raspberries, strawberries)
- 1 tbsp sliced almonds
- 1 tsp stevia or honey (optional)

Instructions:

1. In a bowl or jar, combine chia seeds and almond milk. Stir well to prevent clumping.
2. Let the mixture sit in the fridge for at least 4 hours or overnight to thicken.
3. Before serving, top with mixed berries, sliced almonds, and a drizzle of stevia or honey if desired.

Cooking Time: 5 minutes
Prep Time: 5 minutes (plus chilling time)
Servings: 1

Nutritional Information (per serving):

- Calories: 230
- Protein: 6g
- Carbs: 12g
- Fiber: 10g
- Fat: 18g
- Sugar: 2g

GREEK YOGURT PARFAIT WITH BERRIES AND WALNUTS

Ingredients:

- 1/2 cup unsweetened Greek yogurt
- 1/4 cup mixed berries (blueberries, raspberries)
- 1 tbsp chopped walnuts
- 1 tsp chia seeds (optional)

Instructions:

1. Layer the Greek yogurt in a bowl or parfait glass.
2. Top with mixed berries, walnuts, and chia seeds.
3. Stir lightly and enjoy a creamy, crunchy breakfast parfait.

Cooking Time: 2 minutes
Prep Time: 3 minutes
Servings: 1

Nutritional Information (per serving):

- Calories: 230
- Protein: 20g
- Carbs: 10g
- Fiber: 4g

- Fat: 14g
- Sugar: 5g

AVOCADO & BACON EGG CUPS

Ingredients:

- 2 large eggs
- 2 slices turkey bacon
- 1/4 avocado, diced
- Salt and pepper to taste

Instructions:

1. Preheat the oven to 375°F (190°C).
2. Cut the avocado in half, remove the pit, and scoop out a little of the flesh to create space for the eggs.
3. Place the avocado halves in a baking dish.
4. Crack one egg into each avocado half.
5. Bake for 12-15 minutes, or until the eggs are cooked to your desired consistency.

6. While the eggs bake, cook the bacon until crispy. Crumble the bacon and sprinkle on top of the avocado egg cups before serving.

Cooking Time: 15 minutes
Prep Time: 5 minutes
Servings: 2 (1 avocado half per serving)

Nutritional Information (per serving):

- Calories: 350
- Protein: 20g
- Carbs: 8g
- Fiber: 7g
- Fat: 28g
- Sugar: 2g

These high-protein, low-carb breakfast recipes are designed to fuel your body with the right nutrients to start your day. They're quick to prepare, easy to customize, and will help you stay full and satisfied throughout the morning.

COMPREHENSIVE HIGH-PROTEIN, LOW-CARB LUNCH RECIPES

GRILLED CHICKEN SALAD WITH AVOCADO AND OLIVE OIL DRESSING

Ingredients:

- 4 oz grilled chicken breast
- 2 cups mixed greens (spinach, arugula, lettuce)
- 1/4 avocado, sliced
- 1/4 cucumber, sliced
- 1/4 cup cherry tomatoes, halved
- 2 tbsp olive oil
- 1 tbsp lemon juice
- Salt and pepper to taste

Instructions:

1. Grill the chicken breast until fully cooked (about 5-7 minutes per side). Let it rest before slicing.
2. In a large bowl, combine mixed greens, cucumber, cherry tomatoes, and avocado.
3. Slice the grilled chicken and place on top of the salad.
4. Drizzle with olive oil and lemon juice, then season with salt and pepper to taste.
5. Toss and serve immediately.

Cooking Time: 10 minutes
Prep Time: 10 minutes
Servings: 1

Nutritional Information (per serving):

- Calories: 400 kcal
- Protein: 30g
- Fat: 32g
- Carbohydrates: 10g
- Fiber: 7g

TUNA SALAD LETTUCE WRAPS

Ingredients:

- 1 can tuna (in water, drained)
- 2 tbsp mayonnaise (preferably sugar-free)
- 1 tbsp mustard
- 1/4 red onion, diced
- 1/4 cup celery, diced
- 4 large Romaine lettuce leaves
- Salt and pepper to taste

Instructions:

1. In a bowl, combine tuna, mayonnaise, mustard, diced red onion, and celery. Mix until well combined.
2. Season with salt and pepper to taste.
3. Spoon the tuna mixture onto the center of each lettuce leaf.
4. Wrap up the lettuce around the filling to form a wrap.
5. Serve immediately.

Cooking Time: 5 minutes
Prep Time: 5 minutes
Servings: 1 (4 wraps)

Nutritional Information (per serving):

- Calories: 350 kcal
- Protein: 40g
- Fat: 20g
- Carbohydrates: 6g
- Fiber: 2g

GRILLED SALMON WITH CAULIFLOWER RICE

Ingredients:

- 6 oz salmon fillet
- 1 tbsp olive oil
- 1 tsp lemon zest
- 1 cup cauliflower rice
- 1 tbsp butter
- Salt and pepper to taste

Instructions:

1. Preheat your grill or grill pan to medium-high heat.
2. Brush the salmon with olive oil and season with lemon zest, salt, and pepper.
3. Grill the salmon for 4-5 minutes per side until fully cooked.
4. While the salmon cooks, sauté cauliflower rice in butter over medium heat for 5-7 minutes until tender.
5. Serve the grilled salmon on top of the cauliflower rice.

Cooking Time: 10 minutes
Prep Time: 5 minutes
Servings: 1

Nutritional Information (per serving):

- Calories: 500 kcal
- Protein: 35g
- Fat: 35g
- Carbohydrates: 8g

- Fiber: 4g

CHICKEN CAESAR SALAD (LOW-CARB)

Ingredients:

- 4 oz grilled chicken breast
- 2 cups Romaine lettuce, chopped
- 2 tbsp homemade Caesar dressing (no sugar)
- 1 tbsp Parmesan cheese, grated
- Salt and pepper to taste

Instructions:

1. Grill the chicken breast until fully cooked, then slice it.
2. In a large bowl, combine Romaine lettuce and Caesar dressing.
3. Toss well to coat the lettuce with the dressing.
4. Top with sliced chicken and grated Parmesan cheese.

5. Season with salt and pepper and serve immediately.

Cooking Time: 7-10 minutes
Prep Time: 5 minutes
Servings: 1

Nutritional Information (per serving):

- Calories: 400 kcal
- Protein: 40g
- Fat: 28g
- Carbohydrates: 6g
- Fiber: 2g

BEEF AND BROCCOLI STIR-FRY

Ingredients:

- 6 oz lean beef (flank steak or sirloin), thinly sliced
- 1 cup broccoli florets
- 2 tbsp soy sauce (or coconut aminos for lower-sodium)
- 1 tbsp sesame oil

- 1 tbsp olive oil
- 1 tsp minced garlic
- 1/2 tsp grated ginger (optional)

Instructions:

1. Heat olive oil in a pan over medium-high heat.
2. Add sliced beef and cook for 3-4 minutes until browned.
3. Add broccoli, soy sauce, sesame oil, garlic, and ginger (if using).
4. Stir-fry for another 5-7 minutes until the broccoli is tender.
5. Serve hot.

Cooking Time: 10 minutes
Prep Time: 5 minutes
Servings: 1

Nutritional Information (per serving):

- Calories: 380 kcal
- Protein: 40g
- Fat: 24g

- Carbohydrates: 6g
- Fiber: 3g

TURKEY AND AVOCADO LETTUCE WRAPS

Ingredients:

- 4 oz sliced turkey breast (deli meat or roasted)
- 2 large Romaine lettuce leaves
- 1/4 avocado, sliced
- 1/4 cucumber, thinly sliced
- 1 tbsp mustard or mayonnaise (optional)

Instructions:

1. Lay out the Romaine lettuce leaves and layer with turkey slices.
2. Add avocado slices and cucumber on top of the turkey.
3. Drizzle with mustard or mayo if desired.
4. Roll the lettuce up tightly and serve.

Cooking Time: 5 minutes
Prep Time: 5 minutes
Servings: 1

Nutritional Information (per serving):

- Calories: 300 kcal
- Protein: 30g
- Fat: 18g
- Carbohydrates: 6g
- Fiber: 4g

SHRIMP & AVOCADO SALAD

Ingredients:

- 4 oz shrimp, peeled and cooked
- 2 cups mixed greens (spinach, arugula, lettuce)
- 1/4 avocado, sliced
- 1/4 cup cherry tomatoes, halved
- 1/4 cucumber, sliced
- 2 tbsp olive oil
- 1 tbsp lime juice
- Salt and pepper to taste

Instructions:

1. In a large bowl, combine mixed greens, cucumber, cherry tomatoes, and avocado.
2. Add cooked shrimp on top of the salad.
3. Drizzle with olive oil and lime juice, then season with salt and pepper.
4. Toss gently and serve immediately.

Cooking Time: 5 minutes
Prep Time: 10 minutes
Servings: 1

Nutritional Information (per serving):

- Calories: 350 kcal
- Protein: 35g
- Fat: 25g
- Carbohydrates: 8g
- Fiber: 6g

These 7 high-protein, low-carb lunch recipes are quick, satisfying, and perfect for those looking to maintain or lose weight while still enjoying flavorful meals. They're packed with protein, healthy fats, and fiber, while keeping carbs to a minimum, so you can stay on track with your health goals. Enjoy.

COMPREHENSIVE HIGH-PROTEIN, LOW-CARB DINNER RECIPES

GRILLED SALMON WITH CAULIFLOWER RICE AND STEAMED BROCCOLI

Ingredients:

- 6 oz salmon fillet
- 1 cup cauliflower rice
- 1 cup broccoli florets
- 1 tbsp olive oil
- Salt and pepper to taste
- Lemon wedges (for serving)

Instructions:

1. Preheat the grill or grill pan to medium-high heat.

2. Season the salmon fillet with olive oil, salt, and pepper.
3. Grill the salmon for 4-5 minutes per side, or until cooked through and flakes easily with a fork.
4. While the salmon is grilling, steam the broccoli until tender, about 5-6 minutes.
5. Sauté cauliflower rice in a pan with olive oil over medium heat for 4-5 minutes, stirring occasionally.
6. Serve the grilled salmon with cauliflower rice, steamed broccoli, and a squeeze of lemon.

Cooking Time: 10 minutes
Prep Time: 5 minutes
Servings: 1

Nutritional Information (per serving):

- Calories: 400
- Protein: 35g
- Carbs: 12g
- Fiber: 5g
- Fat: 26g

- Sugar: 4g

CHICKEN THIGHS WITH ROASTED BRUSSELS SPROUTS AND ASPARAGUS

Ingredients:

- 6 oz bone-in, skin-on chicken thighs
- 1 cup Brussels sprouts, halved
- 1 cup asparagus spears, trimmed
- 1 tbsp olive oil
- 1 tbsp garlic powder
- 1 tbsp fresh thyme
- Salt and pepper to taste

Instructions:

1. Preheat the oven to 400°F (200°C).
2. Season the chicken thighs with olive oil, garlic powder, thyme, salt, and pepper.
3. On a baking sheet, toss Brussels sprouts and asparagus with olive oil, salt, and pepper.

4. Place the chicken thighs on the same baking sheet with the veggies.

5. Roast for 30-35 minutes, or until the chicken thighs reach an internal temperature of 165°F (75°C) and the vegetables are tender.

6. Serve the chicken thighs with roasted Brussels sprouts and asparagus.

Cooking Time: 35 minutes
Prep Time: 10 minutes
Servings: 1

Nutritional Information (per serving):

- Calories: 500
- Protein: 40g
- Carbs: 14g
- Fiber: 7g
- Fat: 30g
- Sugar: 4g

BEEF STIR-FRY WITH BELL PEPPERS AND SNOW PEAS

Ingredients:

- 6 oz lean beef (sirloin or flank steak), thinly sliced
- 1 cup bell peppers, sliced
- 1/2 cup snow peas
- 2 tbsp soy sauce (or coconut aminos for a low-sodium option)
- 1 tbsp sesame oil
- 1 tbsp fresh ginger, grated
- 2 cloves garlic, minced

Instructions:

1. Heat sesame oil in a wok or large pan over medium-high heat.
2. Add beef and cook for 2-3 minutes until browned, then remove from the pan and set aside.
3. In the same pan, sauté garlic and ginger for 1 minute until fragrant.
4. Add bell peppers and snow peas, stir-fry for 3-4 minutes until tender but still crisp.
5. Add the beef back to the pan along with soy sauce. Stir to combine and heat through for another 2-3 minutes.

6. Serve immediately.

Cooking Time: 10 minutes
Prep Time: 5 minutes
Servings: 1

Nutritional Information (per serving):

- Calories: 350
- Protein: 35g
- Carbs: 10g
- Fiber: 4g
- Fat: 20g
- Sugar: 5g

GRILLED CHICKEN WITH ZUCCHINI NOODLES AND PESTO

Ingredients:

- 6 oz grilled chicken breast
- 2 cups zucchini noodles (spiralized zucchini)

- 2 tbsp pesto sauce (store-bought or homemade)
- 1 tbsp olive oil
- Salt and pepper to taste
- Parmesan cheese (optional for topping)

Instructions:

1. Grill the chicken breast for 5-6 minutes per side until cooked through and juices run clear.
2. While the chicken is grilling, sauté zucchini noodles in olive oil over medium heat for 2-3 minutes until tender but still firm.
3. Toss the cooked zucchini noodles with pesto sauce.
4. Slice the grilled chicken and serve over the pesto zucchini noodles. Top with Parmesan cheese if desired.

Cooking Time: 10 minutes
Prep Time: 5 minutes
Servings: 1

Nutritional Information (per serving):

- Calories: 400
- Protein: 40g
- Carbs: 10g
- Fiber: 5g
- Fat: 23g
- Sugar: 4g

BAKED COD WITH ROASTED CAULIFLOWER AND SPINACH

Ingredients:

- 6 oz cod fillet
- 1 cup cauliflower florets, roasted
- 1 cup spinach, sautéed
- 1 tbsp olive oil
- 1 tbsp lemon juice
- Salt and pepper to taste

Instructions:

1. Preheat the oven to 375°F (190°C).

2. Season the cod fillet with olive oil, lemon juice, salt, and pepper.
3. Place the cod on a baking sheet and bake for 12-15 minutes, or until the fish flakes easily with a fork.
4. Meanwhile, roast cauliflower florets with olive oil, salt, and pepper at 375°F for 20-25 minutes until golden.
5. In a pan, sauté spinach in olive oil for 2-3 minutes until wilted.
6. Serve the baked cod with roasted cauliflower and sautéed spinach.

Cooking Time: 25 minutes
Prep Time: 5 minutes
Servings: 1

Nutritional Information (per serving):

- Calories: 350
- Protein: 38g
- Carbs: 12g
- Fiber: 5g
- Fat: 18g
- Sugar: 3g

SHRIMP AND AVOCADO SALAD WITH LIME DRESSING

Ingredients:

- 6 oz shrimp, peeled and deveined
- 2 cups mixed greens (arugula, spinach, lettuce)
- 1/4 avocado, diced
- 1/2 cucumber, sliced
- 1 tbsp olive oil
- 1 tbsp lime juice
- Salt and pepper to taste

Instructions:

1. Heat olive oil in a pan over medium heat. Add shrimp and cook for 2-3 minutes per side until pink and cooked through.
2. In a large bowl, toss mixed greens, cucumber, and diced avocado.

3. In a small bowl, whisk together lime juice, olive oil, salt, and pepper to make the dressing.

4. Add cooked shrimp to the salad, drizzle with lime dressing, and toss gently to combine.

5. Serve immediately.

Cooking Time: 6 minutes
Prep Time: 5 minutes
Servings: 1

Nutritional Information (per serving):

- Calories: 320
- Protein: 30g
- Carbs: 9g
- Fiber: 6g
- Fat: 20g
- Sugar: 3g

PORK TENDERLOIN WITH ROASTED GREEN BEANS AND MUSHROOMS

Ingredients:

- 6 oz pork tenderloin
- 1 cup green beans, trimmed
- 1/2 cup mushrooms, sliced
- 1 tbsp olive oil
- 1 tbsp fresh rosemary, chopped
- Salt and pepper to taste

Instructions:

1. Preheat the oven to 400°F (200°C).
2. Season the pork tenderloin with olive oil, rosemary, salt, and pepper.
3. Roast the pork tenderloin in the oven for 25-30 minutes, or until it reaches an internal temperature of 145°F (63°C).
4. While the pork is roasting, toss green beans and mushrooms with olive oil, salt, and

pepper. Roast for 20 minutes, shaking the pan halfway through.

5. Slice the pork tenderloin and serve with roasted green beans and mushrooms.

Cooking Time: 30 minutes
Prep Time: 10 minutes
Servings: 1

Nutritional Information (per serving):

- Calories: 420
- Protein: 40g
- Carbs: 12g
- Fiber: 6g
- Fat: 22g
- Sugar: 4g

These high-protein, low-carb dinner recipes are designed to be quick, satisfying, and easy to prepare, ensuring you have plenty of options to fuel your body with the right nutrients. Enjoy these meals for a healthier lifestyle while keeping your carb intake in check.

CONCLUSION: EMBRACE THE HIGH-PROTEIN, LOW-CARB LIFESTYLE WITH CONFIDENCE

As you've discovered throughout **High Protein-Low Carb Masterpieces**, this approach to eating isn't about deprivation or complicated restrictions—it's about choosing nourishing, flavorful foods that fuel your body while helping you achieve your health goals. By focusing on protein-rich meals and cutting back on carbs, you've tapped into a powerful way to boost energy, manage weight, and feel better both physically and mentally.

Whether you're cooking up a delicious grilled salmon with cauliflower rice or enjoying a hearty chicken stir-fry with bell peppers, each of these meals is designed to not only support your nutritional needs but also satisfy your cravings. And the best part? You don't have to sacrifice taste or enjoyment to stay on track.

The journey to mastering high-protein, low-carb eating is all about consistency, creativity, and finding what works for you. From meal prepping to experimenting with new recipes, the possibilities are endless. It's not about making drastic changes overnight; it's about adopting small, manageable habits that fit seamlessly into your lifestyle.

Remember, this isn't a short-term fix this is a sustainable way of living. You have the tools and the knowledge to create meals that nourish your body, taste great, and keep you feeling satisfied. And as you continue to explore new recipes and refine your approach, you'll gain confidence in the kitchen and in your ability to live a healthier life.

Don't forget that meal planning and preparation are key to your success. By taking the time to plan your meals ahead, you'll ensure that you're always prepared with delicious, protein-packed options that align with your goals. With each meal you prepare, you're not just nourishing your body, you're also taking control of your health and your future.

As you continue on this high-protein, low-carb journey, keep in mind that food is meant to be enjoyed, celebrated, and savored. Take pride in every delicious dish you create, knowing that you're making choices that benefit both your body and mind.

So, whether you're here for weight management, muscle building, or simply to feel your best, **High**

Protein-Low Carb Masterpieces has equipped you with the recipes and knowledge to make every meal a step towards your goals. Embrace the process, enjoy the journey, and let your kitchen be your playground as you create culinary masterpieces that fuel your life.

Here's to the next chapter of your healthy, vibrant, and satisfying high-protein, low-carb lifestyle. The possibilities are endless, and your success is just a meal away. Enjoy every bite.

Printed in Great Britain
by Amazon